Kip Divided

poems by

Les Epstein

Finishing Line Press
Georgetown, Kentucky

Kip Divided

Copyright © 2022 by Les Epstein
ISBN 978-1-64662-927-5 First Edition
All rights reserved under International and Pan-American Copyright Conventions. No part of this book may be reproduced in any manner whatsoever without written permission from the publisher, except in the case of brief quotations embodied in critical articles and reviews.

ACKNOWLEDGMENTS

A special thanks to the journals and anthologies—print and online—in which some of these poems first appeared: *Clinch Mountain Review, Fourth & Sycamore, Smalltalk Review, Rizal Review, Sweater Weather Magazine, Peeking Cat Magazine, Eyedrum Periodical, Pain & Renewal: A Poetry Anthology* (Vita Press), *Burning House Press.*

A special thanks to my family and friends and teaching colleagues for their support over the years—including the spirited support of Brian Counihan, Josh Chapman, Olchar Lindsann and Stephanie Martin.

Publisher: Leah Huete de Maines
Editor: Christen Kincaid
Cover Art: Sarah Jo
Author Photo: Sarah Epstein
Cover Design: Elizabeth Maines McCleavy

Order online: www.finishinglinepress.com
also available on amazon.com

Author inquiries and mail orders:
Finishing Line Press
PO Box 1626
Georgetown, Kentucky 40324
USA

Table of Contents

Schnapps, 1982 1

The Fossil Life 3

Pancake House and Motel 4

Isolation 2020 5

Isolation Part 15 Serenade on Oak 7

Night Nimbus 8

(Odd Musings Weeks into the Great Quarantine) 9

Isolation, Part Eleven: A Moss the Many 10

Days of Matkes or Isolation 2020, Part V 11

Monster in the Windmill 13

Chiller Theater 14

Mail Call 17

Nuts, I Mean 19

Pretzels Before the Moon 22

Fatuity 26

Cheese Ghosts 28

With Shovel 31

Isolation, Part 9: Coffee Filter Salvation 32

For Nancy & Sarah

Schnapps, 1982
For Augusta Spritzer

His pinochle ends at 5:00
When the players—
A meld of scholars and street toughs—
Leave with failed tricks
Curse through the Adirondack pines

Flick cigar soot and shuffle
Inelegantly away to suppers
Of borscht, broccoli
And basted baked chicken
Washed down with hot Lipton Tea
Steamed with only the finest
Echo Lake tap liquescent

Her cup of Schnapps began at 4:00
A spirited shot—
To keep fluid blood and things adenoidal—
Deeply poured sans formality
In a sand stained juice glass

Set beside apple slices
Blanketed by Muenster
And devoured after Nero Wolfe
Cracked another Manhattan Whodunit—
Brilliantly in his Brownstone—
While tending to orchids
And the day's chicken—no salt—
Snaps and sparks away in the oven

She tunes to Quincy at 5:00
As he is on the mortuary case
And downs Schnapps
Tainted by reservoir grit
(And a hint of citrus)
She dreams that the Borscht Belt

Now dead
Was somehow better.

At the far edge
Of a dank lake,
Three eagles
Land carp for a supper

The Fossil Life

What plans shall I make once I am found as a collected skull. Might I trade baseball notes with 4th Millennium paleoanthropologists or should I prepare a statement of misgivings for misbehaving

When I entered earlier years of academic drudgery, which leaves concern as to whether my old noggin preserved my baldness for all times and would its interior still reveal a passion for afternoons operatic

Not to mention Dorothy Hamill but then again can old skulls really laugh at themselves when finally acknowledging having never met Hamill or the ability to carry the right tune

For things truly operatic so then it would be my hope that I will be saved for Halloween settings on porches. Yes, I might be set upon an oak bench. A candle lit in my cranium, and with orange glow through my sockets, children will gawk and quiver at mighty horrors as they stash sweets in bags.

Or perhaps it would be a theater afterlife for me and I might sit upon as that haughty Scottish king upon a spear or wait, even the better, on some rainy afternoon, a dismayed teen will lift my head and say from his bench: Alas! Poor Epstein, What a Mensch!

Will any then look inside my salty flat bones? Will they seek truth behind the American chaos that dogged my later life? Will they ask where I stored my devotion to a wife and daughter? Will they handle me as treasured trophy or place me in warehouse of stranger skulls?

But should anyone ask what really happened all the odd years of my life, then let them floss my fossil teeth, as this is what they will hear: "which moment was best to fear"?

Pancake House and Motel

Counting crushed coffee lids and Cicada shells, little was left to visit in the lot of the Pancake House and Motel. Its griddle cold for months and its Corn Beef Hash special absent from the plates of those armed with iron-cast gastric lines. At the expense of a brief walk you can grab 'Four Hot Dogs for Five Dollars' at Kat's Café and Kitchen or head

across to Rick's Place of Antiques and Junk, where I wish Bogart and Bergman would gather and recall Paris! Where we could hear Sam pluck out that sublime tune again and finally figure out once and for all what his friendship with Louis might entail. But really this is Rick's Place of Antiques and Junk and so all objects hold echoes of romance in silence,

except now there are ten thousand or more Cicadas, with precise pitch, singing in summer concert as an altruistic morning choir now that churches cannot assemble. Theirs is a humming chorus to rival Puccini's Butterfly humming band, a morning explosion of sound gaudier than Hendrix's sweet Fender Stratocaster anthem—that August morning marriage of alder, maple and string and loud magic

like the noon Norfolk and Southern that hoots as it passes Back Creek. There is some movement out there after all. A horned owl was spotted here years ago, perched on a severed telephone post, hugging the corner of a car rental lot. Dreams of griddled cakes begin.

Isolation 2020

Another night in the tank
We all call home
And I fancy 1976 a better year

When my lunch bag
So delightfully smelling like fish
Found itself

Tossed from the Practical Science room
Bag and all

Leaving me
In my cat fur plastered coat
Gasping for the taste of tuna

I could escape the tank
And take peak at the farms
From the edge of Chestnut Ridge

I would be up high
And lament the dearth
Of practical science

Or tuck my neck
In a fur plastered coat
As my remaining shield

Since breathing between friends
Is recommended to be at six feet
(Why is every damn ultimatum left at six feet?)

And consider spending
Another night in the tank
Praising sardines with the cats

So which is a better world:
To be banished for the love of fish
Or starved for the need of communal breath

Isolation Part 15 Serenade on Oak

After all the closings,
Rising lists of Souls winding homeward,
Carolina Wrens still open the morning
With a Blue Ridge standard
Touching on coloratura tones and notes

Craving
One cat blankets you with yellow hairs
A cover of feline remedy for renewed health
And an engine for skull evacuating sneezes

Dropping yellow hairs to warm special places
Your long arms your legs your tiny nose peaking just over a green sheet

A green pear stands at attention
On your plate
Untouched, abandoned

Night Nimbus

It was winter
When your ovation
Arrived from above—

My book of Orwell's dystopian
Nightmares—

Like a toothy stalactite
Delivering globule after globule
To join my paperback stalagmite below.

It was winter
When your feline liquid love
Flowed past whiskers—

On to rattled pages divining
Wretched truth—

While you, paw stamping above as a night Nimbus
Dripping joy after awe
To save, perhaps, citizen Smith from a brutal end.

It was winter,
My beloved fur ball faucet
It was winter.

(Odd Musings Weeks into the Great Quarantine)
Isolation, Part 7

I long to start with the precise drive
Of a swollen Heart
That never flees from my chest
But beats recklessly
For the new moment to say, "Oh!"

The April Peepers, by the way, hum joy
Over the returning garden,
Rising outside my sentinel window
Their staccato contralto pipes:
God! God! God! God! God! God!

But I too wish for a divine "Oh"
One that, says, to, say, a Ruth-like clout
Over a short right field porch:
God! God! God! God! God! God!
Or
Oh! Oh! Oh! Oh! Oh! Oh!
But all such 'Ohs' have been placed on hold.

Now the Nimbostratus Monsters enveloping the valley
Could thump an "Oh" or two
Beethoven, himself, said Oh and Oh what a symphony
Later Whitman called on his captain much the same way.
We saw this in the movies,
Beloved Robin's picture show
And sighed saying, 'Oh....'

Then there is always Nora Lum.

When Nora Lum appears on the screen
I do utter a longer 'Oh' than usual
And when Nora speaks
I feel a pounding rising inside me
Celebrating the birth of a magnificent, unrequited 'Oh'!

Tomorrow it might rain.

**Isolation, Part Eleven:
A Moss the Many**

The moss amasses and the neighbors hate me now that Oaks and Dogwood root their way from curb to house—old brown bones gripping the hill for cats to file their way for greater weaponry.

In Jersey the mounting bodies are packed in sheds so no one will see. It's still cold enough to preserve and growing all that much colder. Hockey arenas ready for body checking.

"How do you know those are Dogwoods," my father once asked. "You can tell from their bark," I replied. He did not laugh and the joke set upon a pile of many dying jokes.

The tallest mountain nearest to my house is called The Poor. In winter the Poor peers over our town as a Virginia Everest. On nearby peaks vintners plot grapes the poor multiply faster than my dead jokes.

Someone should roll out a barrel. I have just the hill to roll by. It's such a hill we might take a ride on that barrel and roll right the hell out of here, past the Poor and Dogwoods roots and the Jersey dead, armed in fleece and cat weaponry, guided by an April gale.

Days of Matkes or
Isolation 2020, Part V

Clad solely in Matkes—

Those stretched-out cotton briefs,
Barely handling the goods—
It remains divinely true:

Ye old Yiddish words
Are still so fun to say

So in blue Matkes
I watch the rain quit at the tick of 9:00
While an empty yellow bus
Moans through at 9:37 sharp
Bringing bags of breakfast
For babes sequestered

Behind windows
Waiting for pancakes
Better tossed as Olympic discs

These are wild faces
Pressed against windows
Desiring to ride once again with a breeze

Like the one winding its way
Over Poor Mountain
And into our bowl of a valley

Breakfast officially ends on Tuesday.
And all will be starved for friends and food
While yards away
One mows over his six feet of solitude

There, beneath the cotton layers of Matkes,
Two estranged fingers reach make a scratch
Soothing agony away without strained mindfulness

It's a Whitman-like flash of the right rear fender—
A fender set to turn sixty next January.

The Sun's up! Hot Damn! It's fucking Tuesday!
I'm gunning for the transcendental.

Monster in the Windmill

"There's a Monster in my Windmill,"
He says and says and says
"Stealing and thrashing all my best humors,"

"There's a Monster in my Windmill,"
He says and says and says,
Believing most of the latest rumors.

He now says and says and says again,
"Then Berra blasted one in the Bronx,"
Holding on to that April from way back when

"Then Berra suddenly blasted one
Way beyond that monster fence."

Chiller Theater

I

Bloodcurdling television nights jumped into force with the vocal arrival of old Fritz, that mustachioed movie host, fashioning himself as the Night Owl, drifting about the Friday night screen in screaming reds and greens. From midnight forward it would be a horned goggled masked Fritz on our Xenith, my father with pistachios ready for Victor von Frankenstein's Monster to rise and fall in lovely black and white.

This is the night of our first horror film—my brother and I—the room's silence invaded by a sickening plopping, a splash of outlandish clicks, setting my ten-year old nerves on edge. I had to tinkle but refused to move; I was ready for whatever Fritz had to show.

More plopping. My father cracked pistachios. He stopped and listened. "Is that the sink," he asked, "dripping and left on carelessly?" It's not the sink he realizes. Fritz finishes his introduction. Music by Kaun raised the three hairs on my arms, Zombie-like tufts in a nocturnal Twist; we would soon see a monster. We quivered. Music and the Plops of the Damned droned.

My father looked for the plopping and returned. "It's the dog," he says. "She's in a corner, licking her knish." We breathed out but then saw the name that we had long heard from children on the rough playground turf: the legend analyzed on foursquare courts. "Boris Karloff," it said, right across the screen.

"Ah, yes, Boris Karloff, The Man of a Thousand Faces," my father boasted. "What," cried my brother? "How can he have a thousand faces," he cried, picturing Boris' faces molting from beast to creature. "Karloff in 'The Body Snatchers,' Stevenson, a scene in the marshes… the coach pulling speeding along with a dead body freshly stolen from its grave for experiments, and up pops the dead man right into view. I remember how we all jumped when Karloff's fantastic face rose. My sister hid under the seats, her dress stuck to the floor by splotches of soda, her hair matted with chewed popcorn that had been spewed out during an earlier showing."

II

That night Nixon chomped at the bully pulpit, Clemente bopped with the sweetest of swings, the Soviets were something to fear, and my father hid his pistachio stash on the highest shelf. I sat on a kitchen floor waiting for the Monster's rise. We launched a thousand questions in gunning fashion: "How does he afford such a big castle?" "I don't know!" "Do doctors like digging up graves?" "No!" "Who pays his electric bill?" "Mrs. Frankenstein." "Does he like baseball? "Probably not." Colin Clive played the doctor. "Why are scientists always mad in the movies," our old man complained? "Why not fanatical plumbers? Someone should make a movie about a maniacal master-plumber concocting ghastly pipes." We witnessed the Victor von Frankenstein sew dead bits—arms and legs and finally a head—to make one giant Karloff—with amazing bolts in his thick neck. Then the Monster lay on the table, a son of a Prometheus destined to run amok. We asked: "His hair! Who cuts his hair?" "I don't know!" "Alive!" Alive!" The mad doctor shouts! "Pee! Pee!" "Where can he go to pee?" "In the castle potty." "If his name is Victor, what did he win?" "Here they call him Henry," he says. "Watch the movie," he insists!

III

Tricky Dick Nixon soon flopped from his pulpit; sad Fate stole dear Roberto away. One boy found his old man's pistachio stash and chewed and chewed, and Henry's fantastical Monster fell into the pit of Ignorance's flames. I swear we saw the Monster chased for tossing tiny Maria like a skipping stone into a tranquil lake. But God only knows not all children can float. We saw death with our bottoms tightly bound on the linoleum floor, while our old man, in horror, drooled pistachio paste from the corners of his mouth. He watched wearing a fabulous khaki goatee.

"Genius!" he said, "cinematic genius!" "Look how James Whale made the mad Monster wail!

Genius! Simply, horrifying genius," as the Monster mindfully sought shelter in that crabby windmill on a hill. There the Monster's history ended. In the height of a bad night... "There he is," shouted one with a pitchfork, "the murderer," and all shouted for blood. The good doctor, Henry, tossed from the top of the Mill, flopped on its rotating blades, and no music played: only hounds howl. The old man sent us off to bed. He said he was never afraid. But we had seen the Monster. So we tossed, turned and imagined grisly matters, Monsters waiting in the Pale to wail.

Mail Call

I

His fashion is an ingenious shuffle, a swaggering swish of feet, a hideously crafty footwork—leaning less and less to the Astaire, with the Nureyev having left his nerves, and all Chaplin having fled his 'shank's pony'; his is an ambulatory mission towards a pillared, metal box

Empty at noon though he imagined tearing through envelopes, seeking postcards happily suggesting better mortgages, greener lawns, hot television deals, sizzling pies with horrific mounds of cheese, lawyers and deals and all signs of Humanity to be found in a pillared, metal box

Empty at 2:00 though he dreamed to study bon mots suggesting dressing salads with cider or milk, color matching colas with juice, jeans sagging off ermine-shaped boys and girls, even notices from "third rate shysters," he prayed for and heading down the drive, no longer certain blessings come from Scotch, Adirondacks, Labradors, or generous doses of Baroque. His were miserable lines towards a pillared, metal box

Empty at 4:00 although—

OLIO
He once walked on his toes,
Sunday Times in tow,
Bouncing to Adirondack beaches,
Where New York men hollered hyena-like
On all things science and Mozarteum:
But his toes are no longer in charge,
Briskness abandoning his sagging barge.

Although then he could voice on
Sunday Puzzle rows
Hobnob in red Adirondack seats,
With side-burned gents swapping Bawdy Jests

Bending Brows high and low to equal size:
But his voice now slurs like a lazy barge
Leaving the girth of Decay viciously in charge

II

He loves that an old red tail on lamppost watches over highway 2-7-0, picturing this beast plucking mice and snakes off the browning lawn he pushes his cracked sneakers over and up his long hill, passing aging canine deposits to a kitchen stocked with mail debris, his nostalgic withholdings forever

Empty having lost all those winks over potboiler espionage hard backs, bought in ports of call like Phoenix, Poughkeepsie, Portland and, after a hot day's rest, never Phoenix again as he is a stumbling player drifting up his own raked driveway, always hawkish over his mail though now there are no calls for his maleness, no clear gateway to love and sex, no reliance on his former nostalgic withholdings forever

Empty at all hours this day though the coming morning will be a Monday morning and all should be fine should it finally rain.

Nuts, I Mean

"Hot sun
Want some?
Nuts, I mean"

"We have Cardinals and Chickadees
He says, "Year round
In my wild scene,"
He says, rattling
From a thick fluid,
Razing his chest

"Chickadees and Cardinals
Year round
In our forest back
Of the house,
Our dense forest,
Of five trees

"Well, of Maples
There were once six
But that squall took the one
Out in January
We rushed home
From the Country
To beat the worst storm
That August
To catch that tree…"

"Hot sun
Want some?
Nuts, I mean"

"I see someone
Bought that house,"

He says,
"With yellow fluid flowing
Past his lips.
"It was empty for two years.
He sold the house
Because she went, you know, Wahoo!"

"Hot sun
Want some?
Nuts, I mean

"Barmy, cracked and screwy
Or how should I say"?
"I think it's still empty.
I don't know that car.
He sold the house
Because she went, you know, Wahoo!"

"We have a deep woods,"
He says,
"In the summer sun
I cannot see the neighbor's houses
In back of this house,
But this winter…

"I see we have
Been visited by
The red-wigged,
Rubber-lipped
Pagliaccio"
He says.
"Many neighbors have set
Wall feeders full of cheers for him—
Others say he will eventually fly off"

"Hot sun
Want some?
Nuts, I mean"

He asks, sitting on
Folding chair,
Its lacquer varnish
Finished by rain and
And the weight
Of his slouching bulk.

Set on his square slab
Overlooking the street
Cornered by palatial stucco
Warmed by a glass door
Catching the sun's best rays—
A Prince of Fade

"Hot sun
Want some?"

Pretzels before the Moon

It's a driving hanker
For salt upon my tongue—
A need for an excellent chew
On severely baked bread—
That rouses my midnight pantry raid

It would only be a quick sneak
In through that
Blasted squealing pantry door
That alarms your salted brain
Out of sleep and away from bed—
Away from your wife of fifty-seven years

"Where's Mom," your lips say,
Trembling like
Strings on a banged upon Les Paul,
Crushed by Townsend
Or even merry, old Paul himself

"It's morning again," you say—
Raw words slurred allegro
With unabashed spit exploding
From your eighty-two year old lips

But here follows silence
After your violent stammer
We gaze face to face
My arm reaching for a taste
Yours leaning to embrace
The pantry door,
Launching another whine.
We gaze face to face
For a minute or two—
Dumbstruck by our fading union—
It's a minute that plays itself as hours

"Pretzel?" I ask,
Hands retreating from the Snyder's tin
"Care to share an old Monk's treat?
A little reward
Before we all cross our arms in
A decent sleep?"

"No!" you say
Since the thrill for food has long since left you

But consider pretzel trivia!
Since small talk
Has quit
As a Holy Deal for this bunch

"It's said the Pilgrims
Met the first Americans with pretzels,
Or that brave Austrian bakers
Once fought off invading armies with pretzels
Adding salt to thousands of Ottoman wounds."

But your arms dangle
Like Townsend's busted strings
Yours a mind—
That once professed faith
Emphatically in polymers—
Now spins like the
Cratered Moon that catches your eye—
Its reflection painting
A false gleam over blued Irises

"Looks like a Harvest Moon," I say,
Dreaming of a jaw full of pretzel,
Longing for the puffed cheeks
Of a squirrel on an autumn hustle

"Why should there be
A harvest of the moon?" you reply.
"For the Swiss cheese,
You once said, that made up the moon
So many years before…
For the best Swiss cheese
In an otherwise callous cosmos"

"Where's Mom," your lips say

"She sleeps
Under the moonlight"

We expect sleet
Will soon spitefully lash the ground

We consider lost
The chemicals that bind and bind

I hanker again
For that Marvelous smack of Mustard
I think I'll be damned
Or we'll have Pretzels before this Moon
Settles away

You fearfully consider
How reach for yet another Moon.

Half past Midnight
And Pretzels drop into the right hands

We chew hard bread
Arms crossed, eyes glazed
I've my squirrel guise
Yours a stunned face,

With salt spraying from your lips
Into the kitchen sky,
Making new stars
For your own briefly-lived constellation

Or a deathly shower of indoor sleet
Nevertheless, the best of evenings
Are spent with Pretzels,
With that right touch of Mustard,
Spicing up the right color for this Moon

Fatuity

Winter argues for its rank:
So a little ice for a Tuesday—
Appears as expected—
Enough to devour white blossoms
Off the Bradford Pears

Enough to seize branches and leaves

And your face sits in like shock—
Cerulean capsules tight in fingertips—
Your wrecked body warming a handsome kitchen
And considering the swallowing of another's pill

Perhaps the right Coffee
Might hasten your Spirit
Out from under
What Chaucer's brothers and sisters
May have called fatuity—
For I am certain I see within you
A rebellion against this glacial

Dissolve of Memory.

What a ferocious bite you have received.
Shadowing looms over your former pleasantries:
DiMaggio and polemics and spouse…
All fade from your catalogue of concerns

If I were a miner
I'd be trepanning your skull
After memories no longer at the ready
For you
Firmly with white-knuckled hold of the kitchen table

Join bowls of tuna and oranges in still life

You do warm the kitchen—
A father Lear grasping at a decision
Should you devour something
Other than creamed wheat
And as evening fades on this wretched diurnal

Only Chenoweth on television remains…

For when she sings
From that 'Miserable' musical
"Bring him home! Bring him home!"
You rise from your shock
And roundly applaud a desperate song sung light

Then as with winter
You struggle for your rank,
Briefly reclaiming your old estate
Forever divided by the enigmatic—
Holding on to Chenoweth's chiming tones:
Should air and circumstance
Suddenly lift you up and away to a finer Lodge.

Cheese Ghosts

Prologue

A man for his sandwich!
I say, again,
A man for his sandwich!

I

With bagel and sausage
Tight in his paws
Here prepares a man for his sandwich.

It's a damn hot sandwich
Microwaved to perfection
With egg and spirited turkey
And mounds and mounds of melted cheddar

It's a damn sloppy sandwich
With faintly cooked egg
Poached fancifully with extreme salt
(Sea salt, please, this diner
Only cooks with sea salt)
Slapped upon inflated dough
That many in these parts
Believe represents the Bagel and Bialy Society

Yet for all the time he considered
Such a breakfast
Much is slipping through his claws.
Bending and twisting towards his plate

This fellow simply cannot hold his cheese.

His eyes beam forward past me
And quite possibly clasps
On the garbage bin behind me

Here is a cheese ghost,
Escaping its toasted binders,
Spindly goo,
An Orange ectoplasm,
A lactose spirit ripping
And winding its way towards
A terra cotta plate,
Hoping to cause some to scream

He nibbles
Yet ignores his potatoes
(Who ignores potatoes?)
And bounds out to the sidewalk
For a smoke between bites,
With cheddar haunting his beard
After all
What is cheese but the ghost of a mother's milk?

II

The snow expected
This afternoon
Will be the second such snow
Since you passed

On as a spirit
Winding away from this terra

It should be a deep snow
Judging by the howl
Pelting the diner,
Its orange awning
Ripped from its ties
And flapping for good measure
To haunt a sandwiched world—
Diner pressed upon diner—
As a disgruntled, chattering ghost

                        Epilogue

It should be a delightful snow
I say, again,
It should be a delightful snow
Offering you one fine extra blanket

With Shovel

Each has a chance with the shovel
Scooping clay to wrap the man away
Though rain styles the Ohio mud thick
Souls resolve by covering where he lays

Isolation, Part 9:
    Coffee Filter Salvation

Clowning up as suburban bandits
We three stumble into the empty park,
Breathing through coffee filters
Tucked away in cotton life-preservers
And there we conduct a baseball season
Tossing, though never catching,
A ball between the rising Violets and Chickweed

Bouncing off ankles and wrists
Our cowhide sphere
Ricochets away in a Blue Ridge wind,
Its red stitches angrily tattooing flesh
Plunking wounds for dinner banter.

God! This is excruciatingly fun.

White county sheriff cars saunter by
Hovering in corners like pale spiders,
Declaring: "No more than 10 bandits per park,"
Though never uttering such syntax.

So we hunker away on our hillside.
Wave to midday dog walkers
Rustle up webby pasta with sauce
And enter the night for a kip divided.

Les Epstein is a poet, playwright, librettist, stage director and educator. His produced plays and libretti include the award-winning children's opera, *Barefoot* (1997) and the folk opera, "*Miss Lucy*," which premiered in 2011. Two plays—*Ruby Plumb* and *Dinner with the Hornblatts*, premiered at the Belfast Maskers Theatre (Maine)—are available through Green Room Press, and his collaboration with Claudia de Franko, *Llorona of the River*, is available through Silver Birchington Plays. Other works staged include *The Window Washer's Wuhan* (Oregon's Astor Street Opry), *Ira's Fantastical Ride up New York 9* (West Virginia's Greenbrier Valley Theater), *Possum Blossom* (Roy Arias Theatre, NYC), and *Thus Slud Zarilla* (Virginia's Page to Stage). In 2018, Cyberwit Publishers released six short plays and the *Miss Lucy* libretto as a collection called *Seven*. Likewise, Epstein's poems have appeared in journals in the United States, Philippines, Ireland, India and the U.K. Recent credits include *Slant, The Bluestone Review, Interstice, Eyedrum Periodically, Jelly Bucket, The Clinch Mountain Review, Mojave River Review*—some of which were featured in the podcast *Sunflower Sutras* broadcast (Washburn University). Les holds BA in Theatre and English from Otterbein College, a master's degree from Miami University and continued his studies at New York University and The Ohio State University (in theater education). He completed his teacher training at Mary Baldwin College in Virginia. He teaches theater and Humanities at the Community High School of Arts & Academics in Roanoke, VA.

www.ingramcontent.com/pod-product-compliance
Lightning Source LLC
LaVergne TN
LVHW041602070426
835507LV00011B/1248